FAMILY LIFE

Stewart Ross

HODDER
Wayland

an imprint of Hodder Children's Books

ANCIENT EGYPT
Family Life
Food and Feasts
Pharaohs
Temples, Tombs and Pyramids

© 2000 White-Thomson Publishing Ltd

Produced for Hodder Wayland by
White-Thomson Publishing Ltd
2/3 St Andrew's Place
Lewes
BN7 1UP

Editor: Liz Gogerly
Design: Stonecastle Graphics Ltd
Consultant: Dr. J. Fletcher
Proofreader: Alison Cooper
Artwork: John Yates
Map Artwork: Peter Bull

Published in Great Britain in 2001 by Hodder Wayland,
an imprint of Hodder Children's Books

Picture acknowledgements
The publisher would like to thank the following for their
kind permission to use their pictures:
AKG, London 11, 15, 19, 22, 24, 26, 29, 30, 34, 36, 37, 41;
Art Archive 6, 10, 13, 14, 21, 25, 32, 33, 35, 39 (top), 40, 42,
45; **Ashmolean Museum** 20; **Dennis Day** 5, 44; **C.M.
Dixon** 17; **Werner Forman** 4, 16, 23, 38, 39 (bottom);
Hodder Wayland Picture Library (contents), 12, 18, 20,
43; **Michael Holford** (cover).

Please note that the language of the quotations in this
book has been translated in a way to make it accessible
to younger readers. The precise date of each quotation
is generally not known.

A Catalogue record for this book is available
from the British Library.

ISBN 0 7502 3264 1

Printed and bound in Italy
by Eurografica S.p.a.

Hodder Children's Books
A division of Hodder Headline Limited
338 Euston Road
London NW1 3BH

CONTENTS

1 A Hunting Trip

It is still dark. The servant Paneb approaches Nakht's bed with an oil lamp. Very gently he shakes the boy awake. Nakht groans and sits up, rubbing his eyes with his fists. Seconds later, he leaps out of bed. Of course! It's the day of the family hunting trip to the marshes. He dashes into the bathroom and sloshes water over his face. After a quick prayer to the household gods, he grabs a piece of bread and runs out of the house towards the river.

The servants have been up for an hour already, getting everything ready in the family boat. Nakht clambers aboard and waits impatiently for everyone else to arrive.

Down the Nile

Nakht's elder sister, Menwi, is helped aboard by her personal servant. A few minutes later his father and mother appear out of the darkness and take their seats in the boat. 'All ready, sir?' calls the captain. Hunefer, Nakht's father, nods and the boat is pushed off into the stream.

To the east, the sky is beginning to lighten with the first colours of dawn. The broad current of the Nile carries the craft swiftly downstream, so there is no need for the crew to row. The captain, standing at the stern, steers with a long oar tied to the side of the boat.

The camp

Hunefer, one of the king's most experienced and trusted merchants, knows the river well. After a couple of hours, he spies a small island surrounded by reeds and marshes over to their left, and tells the captain to steer towards it.

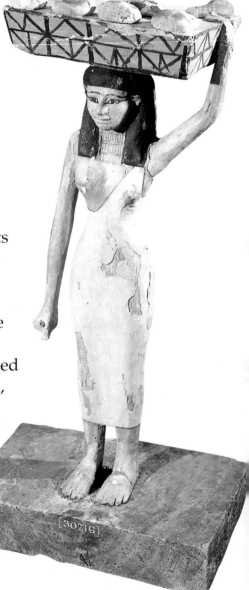

Food for the family – a servant carries a basket of bread and meat neatly balanced on her head. Bread was the staple diet of ancient Egypt.

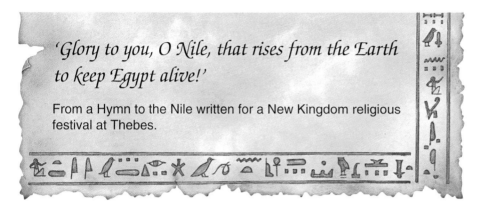

'Glory to you, O Nile, that rises from the Earth to keep Egypt alive!'

From a Hymn to the Nile written for a New Kingdom religious festival at Thebes.

Soon afterwards, when the boat has been pulled up on the bank, the family scramble ashore. Menwi and her mother, Nehesy, supervise the servants as they set up camp. Nakht and his father take their fishing spears out of the boat and set off for a creek at the edge of the island.

Life in the desert – the green banks of the Nile, whose waters enabled the civilization of ancient Egypt to flourish for over 3,000 years.

The picnic

Nakht and Hunefer have no luck. When they get back to the camp, they find Menwi and her mother sitting under a sunshade playing senet on a board of wood and ivory. Beside them, on a rush mat, the servants have set out a meal: bread, figs and grapes, pieces of spicy duck, beans and onions. There is a large jar of beer to drink and a pottery flask of wine from Palestine.

After the meal, Hunefer and Nehesy take a nap. Menwi and Nakht test each other's writing, taking it in turns to draw hieroglyphs in the dry soil with a stick. They then go off with Paneb to explore the island.

A nobleman, armed with a throwing stick, hunts birds in a Nile reed bed. Egyptians hunted for sport and food.

Hunting

When he wakes up, Hunefer glances up at the sun and announces that there is still time for a little hunting. But they'll have to hurry to make sure they get back before it gets dark.

Nakht and his father, armed with their throwing sticks, go to the edge of a reed bed. When Hunefer gives the command, some of the servants start shouting and throwing stones into the reeds.

The noise sends a number of birds, including a huge heron, flapping furiously into the air. But Nakht and Hunefer are not on form. Their sticks whistle harmlessly past their targets and have to be fished out of the river by the servants.

The journey home

When everything has been packed and the family has climbed aboard, the boat is pushed out into the stream. There is now a strong northerly breeze and, when they are clear of the island, the captain orders the sail to be raised. The servants, who would have had to row back against the current, are delighted.

Nakht and Menwi are exhausted and the gentle rocking of the boat soon lulls them to sleep. Paneb covers them with a linen blanket and watches over them until, as a brilliant white moon rises over the river, they finally arrive home.

'Egypt is the gift of her river.'
Herodotus, a Greek historian.

2 Egypt and its People

Menwi, Nakht and their parents lived about 1500 BC, some 3,500 years ago. By that time, the civilization of ancient Egypt was already thousands of years old.

The ancient Egyptian civilization was one of the longest-lasting the world has ever known. Modern researchers believe it began about 5500 BC, when a farming people known as the Badarians settled in Upper Egypt (the south).

MEDITERRANEAN SEA

DELTA

LOWER EGYPT

FAYUM

Giza

Memphis

Saqqara

Dashur

SINAI

River Nile

UPPER EGYPT

el Amarna
(Akhetaten)

Abydos

Dendera

Naqada

Deir el Bahari

VALLEY OF THE KINGS

Karnak, Luxor
(Thebes)

Deir el Medina

N

0   100   200   300 km

0   100   200 miles

Aswan

A map showing ancient Egypt during the New Kingdom (about 1550–1070 BC).

Over the next 2,500 years, two Egyptian civilizations grew up, one in Upper Egypt and one in Lower Egypt (the north, nearest the Mediterranean).

In about 3100 BC, King Menes united the sub-kings and chiefs of Upper and Lower Egypt into a single kingdom with its capital at Memphis. This is when ancient Egyptian history really began.

Three kingdoms

Historians divide the history of ancient Egypt into four main periods. These are the Old Kingdom (about 2690–2180 BC), the Middle Kingdom (about 2055–1650 BC), the New Kingdom (about 1550–1070 BC) and the Late Period (about 747–332 BC). These periods were separated by unsettled times of war and uncertainty, known as 'Intermediate Periods'.

Menwi and her family were fortunate to live at the beginning of the New Kingdom. This was when ancient Egypt was at its most powerful and wealthy. It had a widespread empire and was reckoned to be the mightiest nation in the world.

Thirty-one Dynasties

The ruler at the time Menwi and Nakht went on their trip down the river was King Thutmose I (1504–1492 BC). He was a mighty warrior who fought as far away as Syria. Egyptian merchants like Hunefer, Menwi and Nakht's father, were able to trade safely with distant lands because Egypt's kings were feared and respected.

Between about 3150 and 332 BC, thirty-one families ruled Egypt in succession. Each ruling family is known as a Dynasty. When a king did not have any sons it was sometimes the end of his Dynasty and a new one began. Thutmose I was the third ruler of the Eighteenth Dynasty (often written as Dynasty XVIII). This Dynasty lasted from about 1550–1295 BC.

Continuity ...

One of the most remarkable things about ancient Egyptian civilization was how little it changed over its 3,000-year history. Egyptians like Menwi, Nakht and their parents expected their lives to continue in much the same way as the lives of ancestors had done.

This was partly because Egypt was isolated by sea and desert. Natural barriers made it difficult to invade, so other civilizations had little impact on its way of life. Another reason why it changed so little is that its way of life was based almost entirely upon the regular rhythms of the river Nile. As it rarely changed its behaviour, neither did the people who depended upon it.

Harvest time – crops could be grown only in the fields irrigated by the Nile. The river's annual flood covered surrounding farmland, keeping the soil rich and fertile.

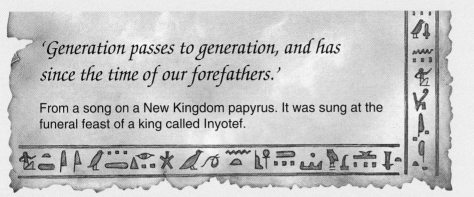

'Generation passes to generation, and has since the time of our forefathers.'

From a song on a New Kingdom papyrus. It was sung at the funeral feast of a king called Inyotef.

... and change

It is wrong, however, to think of ancient Egyptian civilization as completely unchanging. For example, the population of Egypt at the time of Menwi and Nakht was about three million, which was double the number of inhabitants of the Old Kingdom. More people meant more villages, and more land to be cultivated for food. Most upper class families, like Hunefer's, lived in towns. We cannot be certain, but probably about 5–10 per cent of the population in the New Kingdom were city dwellers.

As the Egyptian empire grew, other ideas and goods entered the country from outside. Successful wars, for example, usually meant more slaves. The slaves attached to Hunefer's household, like the faithful Paneb, may well have been descended from men and women captured in war.

War and empire made Egypt rich. The lifestyle enjoyed by Hunefer's family in the sixteenth century BC was more lavish than that enjoyed by their ancestors. In earlier times, the wine from Palestine that they took on their picnic would have been enjoyed only by the king and his family and a handful of wealthy nobles.

Assisted by her servants, a noblewoman tries on her lotus necklace. All the women are wearing traditional heavy eye make-up and wigs.

The fertile strip

The lives of the Egyptians were directly linked to the river Nile. Indeed, without the river there would have been no ancient Egyptian civilization. It flourished only in the narrow strip of fertile land that bordered the river and broadened into a delta where the Nile entered the Mediterranean. On either side lay arid desert.

The desert, which was level and sandy to the west, rocky and mountainous to the east, was Egypt's natural protection. An enemy army could threaten the country only across the sea from the north or across the cataracts (rapids) and mountains to the south. Ancient Egypt was not seriously threatened from either direction until after 1000 BC (the first millennium BC).

Three seasons

An Egyptian's year closely followed the river's three phases. Between February and June, the river ran low and Egypt was in drought. This was when Hunefer and his family made their trip, as the current was slow and safe.

Lost fertility – a field beside the Nile made barren by salt brought to the surface by the river's annual flood.

This was also the time of harvest, when most men and many women worked in the fields.

When the rains fell in the southern Highlands in central Africa, usually beginning some time in June, the river rose rapidly. It flooded the fields that lay along its banks. In a bad year it rose even higher, washing away whole villages. A season of low rainfall was just as harmful because it left much farmland without irrigation. When the river was in flood, most Egyptian men worked on building projects, and Hunefer had to make sure the royal boats were carefully secured to stop them being swept away. The floods had gone down by October. As the farmland emerged from the waters, it had to be marked out again before being planted for the new crop. Farmers also worked hard at this time to store as much of the floodwater as possible in man-made canals, ponds or basins.

A wife sows new seed as her husband ploughs the land (top). Later in the year he cuts the corn with a sickle, ready for her to gather (bottom).

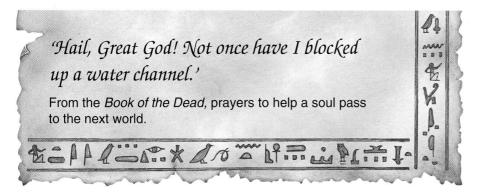

'Hail, Great God! Not once have I blocked up a water channel.'

From the *Book of the Dead*, prayers to help a soul pass to the next world.

Ships, mud, fish and reeds

As well as being the main source of water for drinking, washing and irrigation, the Nile had many other uses. It was a central highway, linking together the different regions of a kingdom that was over 1000 km long. Mud from the river bank was turned into pottery or moulded and dried in the sun to make bricks. Fish from the Nile made a nutritious and tasty meal.

The Egyptians were expert at using the papyrus that grew beside the Nile. They wove the stalks into all sorts of household objects, such as mats, baskets and sandals. They also learned to make a type of paper (papyrus) out of strips of stalk beaten together. The records of Hunefer's deals were kept on rolls of papyrus.

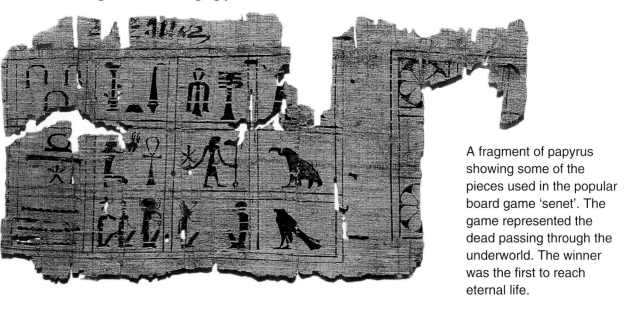

A fragment of papyrus showing some of the pieces used in the popular board game 'senet'. The game represented the dead passing through the underworld. The winner was the first to reach eternal life.

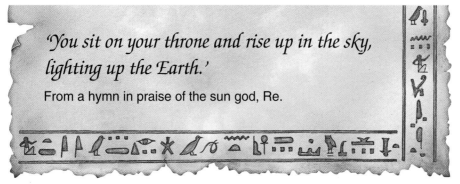

'You sit on your throne and rise up in the sky, lighting up the Earth.'

From a hymn in praise of the sun god, Re.

The king ...

As in a modern country, Egyptian society was divided into many different groups or classes. At the top stood the king and the royal family.

The king of Egypt was more than just a ruler. Egyptians believed he was the son of Re, the sun god. If he was not worshipped as a god during his life (historians are unsure), then he certainly became one when he died. He owned everything and was in charge of everything, from worship to irrigation.

Towards the end of the New Kingdom, kings were called 'pharaoh'. This originally meant 'great house' – the royal palace. As it is confusing to call some rulers 'king' and others 'pharaoh', it is simpler (although less romantic) to call them all just 'king'.

... and his people

It was clearly impossible for the king to carry out all his tasks himself. He was helped by numerous officials. The most important was the vizier, a sort of prime minister. Beneath him were priests, and administrators, scribes (clerks skilled at writing), officers and soldiers, skilled workers and servants.

Two forms of the sun god. On the left he is Atum, 'The All'; in the middle he is the falcon-headed Re.

Taxation

There was no money in ancient Egypt, although gold and other precious metals were sometimes used as payment. Hunefer traded on behalf of the king – many merchants were royal servants – by barter (swapping). Normally, workers were paid and taxes collected in the form of things used in everyday life, such as grain, hides, meat and cloth. There is a record from around 1170 BC of workers going on strike because they had not been paid their meals!

All under control

Royal servants like Hunefer were rewarded with food, goods and valuables from the royal stores. These stores were filled with grain, minerals from the royal mines and taxes collected from the people. To organize this, the land was divided into forty-two provinces, known as 'nomes'.

Each nome was looked after by a royal overseer. He was responsible for working out how much land was cultivated each year and collecting taxes accordingly.

Time to be counted – a farmer brings his cattle before royal tax collectors (holding sheets of papyrus). As there was no money in ancient Egypt, wealth was measured in possessions of all kinds.

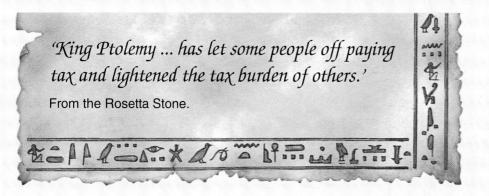

'King Ptolemy ... has let some people off paying tax and lightened the tax burden of others.'

From the Rosetta Stone.

In a year of heavy flood, for example, crops could be planted over a wider area than in a drought year. The government even had Nilometers to measure the height of the water!

Families rich and poor

Obviously, the lives of different families varied a good deal. Hunefer's family, for example, lived in much greater comfort than that of a typical farmer. No other ancient Egyptians enjoyed anything like the luxury of the king and his family.

Nevertheless, most Egyptian families had much in common. They shared the same beliefs. They wore much the same style of clothes and enjoyed similar food and games. Above all, they all valued family life very highly and regarded their children as blessings from the gods.

A picture from the Middle Kingdom shows the nobleman Imnhat and his family in front of an offering table laden with food.

3 At Home

Broadly speaking, there were three types of house in ancient Egypt: palaces, villas and simple houses. Because palaces were large and well-built, archaeologists have a reasonable idea what they were like. We have a fair idea what villas looked like, and know a little about the cottages of the poor workers because a few have survived.

Wood was scarce and stone was expensive. The usual building material for all types of house was mudbrick, or 'adobe'. This was either made into bricks or just piled up to form a wall. The simplest houses were one storey high, but some town houses had two storeys and a cellar. The flat roofs were used as cool sleeping areas in the summer – just as they are today.

Royal palaces

Royal palaces had dozens of rooms because the king, his family (including several wives) and courtiers all needed somewhere to sleep, wash, dress, eat and receive visitors. Beside these smaller rooms there were airy halls, courtyards with pools of water and a throne room where the king made public appearances. A royal palace was the king's administrative headquarters as well as his home.

The royal scribe Nakht and his wife worship the gods Osiris and Maat in their garden. Underneath the shady trees there is a pond.

Villas and cottages

One of the best-preserved ancient towns is Akhetaten (also known as el Amarna), between Thebes and Memphis. It was built by King Akhenaten in about 1350 BC and then abandoned after he died.

The site had three types of house. The smaller houses had four rooms, one at the front, one in the middle and two at the back. The window openings were high in the walls to help keep the rooms cool. A staircase led to upper rooms or the flat roof. There were also back-to-back hovels where the workers lived.

'Egypt has more to wonder at than any other land.'

Herodotus, an ancient Greek historian.

The larger houses, known as villas, were much grander. They had more than twenty rooms centred around a lofty hall set with columns. Some of the villas had walled gardens with pools, flowers and storerooms.

Deir el Medina – an ancient housing estate. These are the remains of the village which housed the workers who carved the royal graves in the Valley of the Kings.

Decoration

The walls of workers' houses were just smooth mud or brick, with hardly any decoration at all. Better-off families cheered up their homes with wall hangings and coloured tiles on the floor.

No effort was spared in the decoration of palaces and the larger villas. The few wall paintings that survive are artistic masterpieces. The walls and floors of the Great Palace of Queen Nefertiti at Akhetaten were covered with lively scenes from nature, showing the river Nile and a variety of Egypt's birds, animals, trees and plants.

One of the most amusing pieces of decoration fringed the pool of the Great Palace. Here, King Akhenaten had an artist paint symbolic figures representing his enemies, so whenever he strolled around the pool he walked all over his enemies!

Gardens

Pictures show the larger villas surrounded by high walls. Within the walls there was usually a formal garden where the family could rest and take exercise, hidden from the gaze of the common people.

A decorative glass tile inlaid with the eye of the Egyptian sky god, Horus.

A wall painting from a house in el Amarna shows the daughters of King Akhenaten (18th Dynasty) chatting together in the shade.

Every garden had a pool, stocked with several varieties of fish and duck. Around the pool grew shady trees such as sycamores and date palms. Sweet-smelling flowers and shrubs added to the general air of beauty and comfort.

Furniture

The furniture in the simplest homes was nothing more than brick benches, a stool or two and perhaps a low table. Stools with either three or four legs were the most common piece of furniture. They were found in almost every family home, from the royal palace to the workers' houses. The better ones were made of wood with woven seats.

The family's goods, clothes and valuables were stored in chests or baskets. Most homes had some form of light, usually just a bowl of oil with a wick in it. The smartest villas had beds with wooden frames, matting bases and hard pillows of wood or stone.

A painted wooden chest from the New Kingdom. Protected by Egypt's dry climate, it has survived for about 3,000 years.

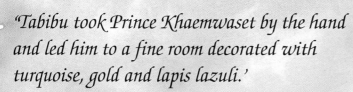

"Tabibu took Prince Khaemwaset by the hand and led him to a fine room decorated with turquoise, gold and lapis lazuli.'

From the New Kingdom tale, *Khaemwaset and the Mummies.*

Soap and a shave

Egyptians made great efforts to keep themselves as clean
as possible. They washed daily, either from a basin at
home or by dipping in the river. The better off took
showers – slaves or servants pouring jugs of water over
them. Large villas had washrooms with toilets and drains.
Ordinary households tipped their sewage into a pit or
straight into the river.

For soap, the Egyptians used a type of perfumed
cream made of oil and lime. After washing they liked
to rub themselves with perfumed oil. As head lice were
a real problem in the hot North African climate, both
men and women often shaved their heads or cut their
hair really short. Men usually shaved their faces or
occasionally wore small beards.

Ancient craftsmanship – a
wood and ivory make-up
jar in the form of a servant
holding a huge container
on his shoulders.

Kilt and sandals

The Egyptians were not as concerned as we are about
nakedness. Children, male and female servants, slaves
and people taking exercise often wore no clothes at all.
Before the New Kingdom men wore just a white linen kilt
tied at the waist. At work they wore a loin cloth. Most
went barefoot. Only the upper classes wore sandals,
which were made of leather or woven reeds and tied
up with leather straps.

By the time of Menwi and Nakht, noblemen's clothing
was changing. Many now wore a long, pleated skirt over
their kilt. On their upper body they wore a sort of small
cloak or cape that covered the shoulders.

Simple elegance

Like men's dress, women's clothes changed
during the New Kingdom. Before then they
wore a plain, full-length dress held up with
shoulder straps.

From about 1500 BC, women started wearing
more elegant and colourful clothes.

They appeared in long, flowing dresses with pleats and fringes. While plain white was still popular, garments in stripes and other colourful patterns were not uncommon. They were probably influenced by the foreign styles that were now making their way into Egypt.

In this family, the children are naked while their parents wear flowing white gowns. The children have partly shaved heads with curls of hair at the side called the 'side-lock of youth'.

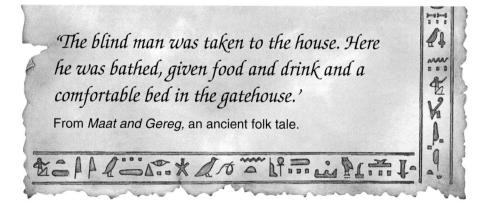

'The blind man was taken to the house. Here he was bathed, given food and drink and a comfortable bed in the gatehouse.'

From *Maat and Gereg*, an ancient folk tale.

The bread of life

Bread was the staple food of ancient Egypt. The Egyptians were fond of livening up their bread with fruits and spices. Popular flavourings included sesame seeds and butter. More than three dozen varieties of bread have been identified.

Market gardens provided a wide range of fruits and vegetables. Sweetness came from fruits and honey, and no feast was complete without dishes of fresh figs, melons, grapes and dates. Popular vegetables included beans, lentils and onions.

Food was cooked over an open fire or in a clay oven. Most cooking utensils were made of pottery. Metal pots were found only in the kitchens of smart villas.

A successful catch – hunters haul in a net full of wild geese.

Pelican and pork

Meat was a luxury dish not often enjoyed by the poorer classes. But as we saw in Chapter One, the wealthy ate all kinds of creatures, even pelican. Beef, mutton and pork were more common, as were pigeon, goose and duck.

Almost everyone ate fish and it was an important source of protein in the Egyptian diet.

Alcoholic drinks

As well as water, milk and juices, the Egyptians also drank beer and wine. Beer was quick and easy to make and extremely popular with all classes. It was brewed at home from barley loaves and dried grain.

Wine was the drink of the wealthy. The grapes were picked and then trampled in large vats to get the juice out. As the Egyptians had not discovered the process of glass-making, the juice was fermented and stored in pottery jars. By the time of the New Kingdom, wealthy Egyptians (like Hunefer) served wine imported from the eastern Mediterranean as well as home-produced wines.

The royal scribe Ani, Overseer of the Granaries, is brought a drink by one of his servants. The table next to him is piled high with fruit and other food.

'When sitting at the table of a nobleman, take only what he gives you.'

Advice to a young man given in the Instruction of the Vizier Ptahhotep.

Dawn to dusk

Compared with the hectic lives most of us lead in the twenty-first century, the daily routine of an Egyptian peasant farming family was slow and uncomplicated. To understand what it was like, try to imagine a world without all modern communications, transport, electricity, machines, medicine, money and materials. The important things were simple and regular: the rising and setting of the sun, the flow of the river, seed time and harvest, and the eternal cycle of birth, marriage and death.

A New Kingdom painting shows farmers working with simple hand-held tools. The days were long and the work was hard.

The day began at dawn. As there were no clocks, people were skilled at telling what part of the day it was from the position of the sun. Adults woke with the sunrise. After washing and dressing, the family ate a simple breakfast of bread and fruit, with water to drink.

Off to work

After breakfast, the father went to work in the fields. In the flood season he might well live away from home while working on one of the king's building projects. He didn't mind this because he was honoured to serve his king. Besides, he was well paid in supplies from the royal stores.

Children helped their fathers in the fields or went fishing. Younger children stayed at home with their mother. She went about her daily tasks, spinning and weaving, collecting water from the river or a well in earthenware jars, making bread and brewing beer.

And so to bed

The midday and evening meals were similar: bread, fruit and perhaps vegetables or a little dried fish. It was washed down with home-made beer.

After dark, the family might sit chatting with neighbours by the light of the moon and stars. They used their oil lamp sparingly because their supply of oil was limited. An hour or two after sunset, after a long day's work, they were glad to get to bed.

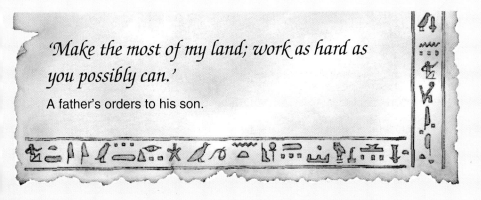

'Make the most of my land; work as hard as you possibly can.'

A father's orders to his son.

Ancient optimists

So much of what we know about ancient Egypt comes from their magnificent tombs. This can give the impression that the Egyptians were a gloomy people, obsessed with death. In fact, the opposite is true.

They held the optimistic belief that death was just a passing from one life to another. That is why they placed everyday objects in their tombs, ready for use in the next world. Other evidence supports the view that they were a cheerful, fun-loving people, ever ready for a game or a party with dancing.

Water sports

As we saw with Hunefer's family, the Nile played an important part in the Egyptians' leisure activities. They swam, held boat races, went on trips, fished, and hunted in the marshes for birds and even dangerous crocodiles and hippopotamuses.

Noblemen hunted in the desert, too. Common targets were wild cattle, foxes, hares, ostriches and hyenas. For centuries they went on foot, stalking their prey and shooting at them with bows and arrows. This changed in the New Kingdom when hunters rode on horseback or in horse-drawn chariots. Camels, which we now automatically associate with Egypt, did not appear until the seventh century BC.

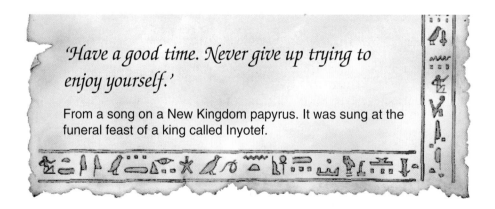

'Have a good time. Never give up trying to enjoy yourself.'

From a song on a New Kingdom papyrus. It was sung at the funeral feast of a king called Inyotef.

Concert time – an elderly musician plays the harp and sings to entertain Inherka the master builder and his wife.

Parties, festivals and games

The wealthy were regular party-goers. The hosts provided plentiful food and livened up the proceedings with music, dancing and other entertainment. Dancers leaped about semi-naked to the sound of lutes and harps. Professional singers, jugglers and acrobats added to the fun, and ample supplies of wine and beer made sure that the guests had a really good time.

The workers could not afford lavish parties, but they did enjoy public festivals in honour of some of the gods. The festival of the cat goddess Bastet, when nobody worked and crowds paraded through the streets, was especially popular.

Those who enjoyed quieter forms of entertainment played board games or read (a limited pastime as only one per cent of the population was literate). For children there were colourful toys, balls and dolls.

4 The Family

The ancient Egyptians had great respect for the family. The unit of father, mother and children was the basis of their way of life. The father was the head of the household. A woman's position in society depended on the status of her father and, after she was married, the status of her husband.

Nevertheless, unlike in many ancient civilizations, women were not second-class citizens. A marriage was seen as a true partnership – the man was responsible for earning to keep the family alive and well, while the woman was responsible for all that went on in the home.

Many Egyptian sculptures and paintings show married couples sitting side by side, sometimes with their arms round each other. The message is clear: their relationship was one of affection and co-operation.

A painted sculpture of a family group from the New Kingdom period. The mother – seated second from the left – is much smaller than her husband who is represented twice on the right.

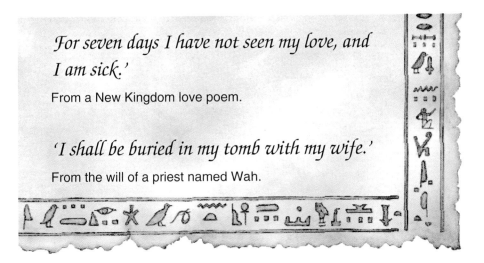

For seven days I have not seen my love, and I am sick.'

From a New Kingdom love poem.

'I shall be buried in my tomb with my wife.'

From the will of a priest named Wah.

Marriage

All men and women were expected to marry. As far as we know, there was no special wedding ceremony or religious service. A marriage began when a couple set up house and lived together.

Most couples married very young. Most girls were generally married between twelve and fourteen, and boys when they were around two years older. Menwi was still single at the age of sixteen – obviously her father and mother had not yet found the right man for her!

Children and divorce

The normal arrangement was monogamy: a man having one wife. Only kings (who had many wives) and a few nobles broke this custom. Children were greatly treasured and couples tried all kinds of things to help them have children. They prayed to gods and goddesses, wrote letters to their dead relatives, took health-giving potions and sometimes even employed magic.

Couples who failed to have children often split up. They might also split up if one of them had an affair with someone else. There was no legal divorce, but families, friends and neighbours usually made sure that men and women did the right thing by each other.

Women and the law

Women were not inferior to their husbands and were in no sense part of his 'property'. In a law court, for example, women were treated the same as men – they could be tried, or bring a case against someone, or act as a witness just as men could.

Nor did women have to depend on their husbands for wealth or property. The law said that a married couple's property belonged to both husband and wife. When parents died, their wealth was shared equally between all their children, male and female. Husbands often left their goods to their wives, too. So a number of fortunate ancient Egyptian women grew rich and powerful in their own right.

Women at work

Noble women did not do manual work but they were kept busy supervising the household. This involved keeping an eye on servants and slaves, planning meals and feasts, hiring extra workers when needed and looking after the house and garden.

Before the New Kingdom, a few educated women served as priests. There is evidence, too, of better-off women trading under their own name. Poorer women did manual work of all different kinds.

Mothers with young children generally stayed at home to look after the family. At busy times they might go and help in the fields alongside the men and childless women. Young girls could find employment as singers, dancers and servants in wealthy households.

Battered beauty – the head of a priestess who was also the wife of Nakhtmin, a prince who commanded the army in the New Kingdom period.

Queen Hatshepsut, the most famous female pharaoh, is shown wearing the royal false beard in this statue on her temple at Deir el Bahari.

Pharaoh Hatshepsut

Without doubt the most remarkable Egyptian woman was Queen Hatshepsut, one of only five female pharaohs. She was the daughter of King Thutmose I and married to her half-brother, Thutmose II. When he died, his child Thutmose III was only a young boy, so Hatshepsut took control of the government.

Some time afterwards, she called herself king and started wearing the costume of a pharaoh, including a false beard! She ruled for some twenty years, erecting magnificent monuments and leading the nation through a period of prosperity and glory.

"Everything my brother gave me, I leave to my wife Teti.'

From the will of a priest named Wah.

Precious infants

Childbearing was extremely dangerous for both mother and baby. A mother's death during or after childbirth was quite common. Between 30 and 40 per cent of children died of disease before their sixth birthday. Consequently, they were not accepted as full members of the community until it was clear they were likely to survive.

Producing a child was the most important thing a woman could do. Childbirth gave her a special position in society because it made sure Egyptian civilization would continue into the next generation. As a result, many paintings and sculptures of women, both wives and mothers, show them as powerful figures who commanded respect.

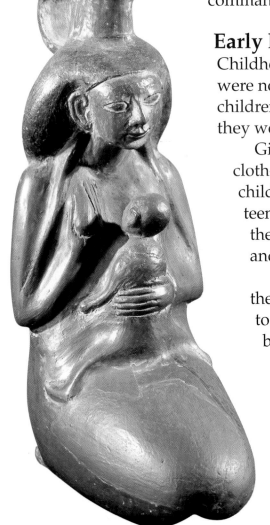

Early learning

Childhood was much shorter than today and teenagers were not thought of as a special group. From an early age children started learning from their parents the skills they would need in later life.

Girls learned household skills, such as baking and cloth-making. Older girls helped look after the younger children. They had to learn fast because by their early teens most girls were married and raising families of their own. By thirty, exhausted by many pregnancies and non-stop work, they were well into middle age.

By about the age of nine or ten, boys accompanied their fathers to work. Before that they were expected to help out with light tasks such as fishing. Some became apprentices, helping in the workshop of an expert and learning his craft. Whatever they did, by fifteen a boy was seen as a young man.

The image of mother and child, so important in ancient Egypt, is here turned into a small jar, or phial, from the New Kingdom period.

School

Privileged boys might go to a scribe school, where they learned to read and write. This, and attending classes given by temple priests, guaranteed them a good job later on. The very wealthy sometimes hired home tutors for their children.

Girls did not generally go to school and historians are not sure how many of them learned to read and write. Like Menwi, they might have been taught by their fathers and brothers. A few messages seem to have been written by women.

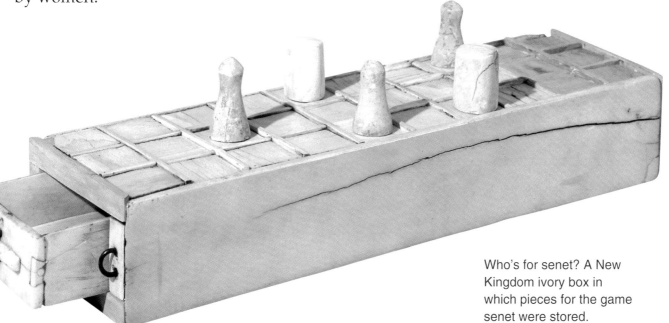

Who's for senet? A New Kingdom ivory box in which pieces for the game senet were stored.

'Rameses the Great, Lord of All the Lands, married the Princess Bakhtan and made her the Great Royal Wife, second in power only to the king himself.'

From *The Princess and the Demon*, about 200 BC.

Slaves

Like all ancient civilizations, the Egyptians used slave labour. The slaves were not their own people but foreigners for whom the Egyptians had little respect. Many were dark-skinned Nubians from the south. Others had been soldiers in armies that the Egyptians had defeated.

Victorious kings and generals brought back slaves from their campaigns in the Middle East. Slaves were also acquired through trade. Egyptian merchants, like Hunefer, would sail to a trading port in Syria, Palestine or North Africa. There they would exchange their cargo of food, precious metals or minerals for slaves, and then return home with the live cargo.

By the New Kingdom, Egypt's army numbered some 40,000 men. This put a huge strain on the country as it took men away from other work. To fill the gap, more slaves than ever were bought or captured. Some were trained as soldiers, while others were sent to work on buildings or in the mines.

What a headache! This bronze statue from the New Kingdom period shows a sick man, possibly a slave, holding his head in pain.

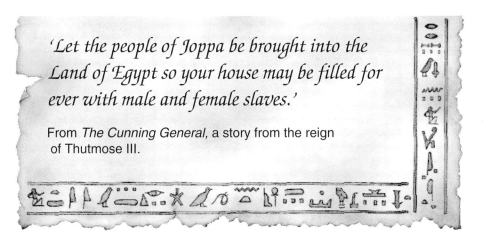

'Let the people of Joppa be brought into the Land of Egypt so your house may be filled for ever with male and female slaves.'

From *The Cunning General*, a story from the reign of Thutmose III.

Worked to death

The work slaves were required to do varied a lot. The hardest labour was in Egypt's copper and gold mines in Nubia, the Sudan and Sinai. Here, watched over by harsh overseers, they worked from sunrise to sunset in the blistering heat with hardly a drop of water to quench their thirst. In these harsh conditions thousands died of sickness and cruelty.

In contrast, slaves who joined a royal palace or a wealthy household could live quite comfortable lives. Nakht's slave, Paneb, for example, was well fed and clothed and treated as a valued family servant.

Wall paintings showing builders at work. Egypt's great monuments were not built by slave labour, as was once thought, but by ordinary Egyptians working for wages.

The horn-headed goddess Hathor is shown lavishly made up with kohl and a striped wig.

Medicine

The Egyptians believed health was a gift from the gods. Sickness came about when evil spirits invaded the body. Because these spirits were thought to behave like little people, they could be got rid of by giving them something really nasty. These 'medicines' (revolting mixtures of things like dung and earth) were put into any of the body's openings.

Egypt was also the first civilization to study rational or scientific medicine. One document, the Edwin Smith Surgical Papyrus, lists forty-eight injuries and discusses how they can be treated. Other documents deal with non-magical medicines. By 1000 BC, Egyptian doctors were regarded as the best in the world.

Beauty treatment

All Egyptians wore make-up. The most common was kohl, an eye liner, made by grinding up a black lead ore and mixing it with oil. It was applied heavily to the upper and lower eyelids with a stick. They also used red ochre to colour the lips and cheeks, and henna for the fingernails.

Wigs were fashion statements, especially at important occasions. Perfumes were made from oil or grease scented with flowers or fragrant woods.

'Oil your skin only with the best beauty products.'
From a medical text written on papyrus.

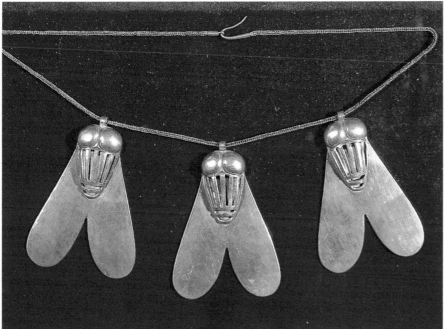

Kamose and his brother Ahmose awarded this necklace of three golden flies to their mother, Queen Ahhotep, for the part she had played in the wars against the Hyksos.

Jewellery

Jewellery was worn by men and women. It made them look good and – as charms or amulets – helped ward off evil spirits. The most popular types of jewellery were rings, bracelets, armlets, earrings (worn through pierced ears) and anklets. The wealthy wore necklaces and sparkling collars.

Like today, those who could afford it wore jewellery made of gold or silver. They did not have access to the precious stones we wear, such as diamonds and sapphires. Instead, their favourite minerals were amethyst, turquoise, lapis lazuli, garnet and onyx. The poor made their jewellery from a highly glazed blue pottery known as faience. Archaeologists have also found jewellery made from shells.

This Egyptian king wears jewellery and a head-dress. Jewellery often showed pictures of the gods.

King Akhenaten, shown here with his beautiful Queen Nefertiti and some of their daughters. He made worship of one god – the sun disc (shown in the background) – Egypt's official religion.

Religion and the world

Religion was vital to every Egyptian, from the mightiest king to the lowliest worker. Egyptians believed the gods and goddesses affected their daily lives at every turn.

Everything an Egyptian family did had a religious aspect. Just as we turn to science to explain the world about us, so the Egyptians turned to their many deities. The sun, for example, was a display of the sun god Re, who travelled through the underworld every evening and was born again each morning. Similarly, the annual drought was a sign of the death of the god Osiris who was miraculously reborn when the floods came.

At home with the gods and goddesses

Egyptian homes had a special area set aside for worship.
The gods most commonly connected with family life were
Bes and Taweret. They were connected with pregnancy
and childbirth. They also helped to keep evil spirits away.
Images of them appeared all over the house, on chairs,
beds and even make-up jars.

Hathor, the goddess of fertility, was another deity
closely connected with family life. The Egyptians
presented little carved female figures at her shrine. These
were either to thank her for the safe arrival of
a child, or a gift in the hope that she would help them to
have a child.

Warding off evil

The Egyptians believed that misery and ill-health were
brought about by evil spirits or angry ancestors. For this
reason it was important for a family to keep on the right
side of their dead ancestors. They kept images of them in
the house and honoured them with gifts.

Evil spirits could be warded off by magic spells that
called on the power of a protecting deity. Magic potions
were also used. So were amulets – charms in the shape of a
friendly deity which were worn round the neck.

'In a dream the princess was shown herbs and
leaves growing beside the Nile. From these she
could make a potion that would help her
become pregnant.'

From the New Kingdom saga, *Se-Osiris.*

Beetle worship – Isis
and her sister, the ancient
goddess Nephthys,
worship the scarab beetle,
which was another form
of the sun god Re.

5 Uncovering Ancient Egypt

The civilization of ancient Egypt did not suddenly collapse. But from about 1070 BC onwards its history became more troubled. Periods of peace and prosperity, sometimes lasting two or three generations, were broken up by internal squabbles and violent foreign invasions.

First, government split between the delta region and the Nile valley to the south. Then the rulers of the delta divided, making prosperous Egypt a tempting target for foreign conquerors. The Nubians swept in from the south, then Assyrians and Persians from the north and east. Finally, with the conquest by Alexander the Great in 332 BC, the civilization of ancient Egypt was broken and a new era in Egyptian history began.

New interest

Under Greek and Roman influence, life in Egypt changed. Visitors wondered at the majestic monuments – the pyramids, temples and palaces – and did much to preserve them from vandalism and natural decay.

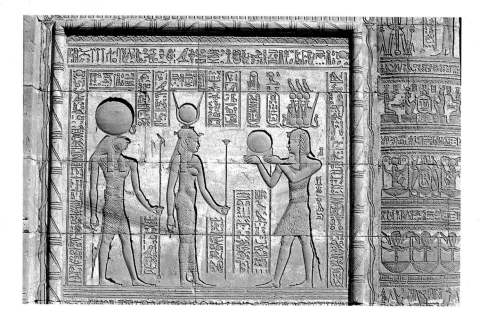

The Egyptian legacy – a Roman emperor, shown as a pharaoh, makes an offering to the goddess Hathor (with horns) and the falcon-headed god Horus.

It was only when the Romans became Christians and closed down the temples that damage was done. As the centuries passed, Egypt's ancient civilization became more mysterious.

During the Renaissance, Western travellers and historians began to take fresh interest in ancient Egypt. This interest grew in the eighteenth century and received a further boost when Napoleon invaded Egypt in 1798. This led to the most important advance in our understanding of ancient Egypt, the discovery and deciphering of the Rosetta Stone in 1822.

Collectors and scholars

During the nineteenth century, scores of priceless Egyptian works of art were packed off to Europe and America. At the same time, archaeologists were starting to uncover the civilization's hidden treasures. The highlight came in 1922, when Howard Carter discovered the tomb of Tutankhamun.

The 1950s and 1960s saw a further flurry of activity. Archaeologists rushed to excavate sites in southern Egypt before they were flooded by the waters behind the new Aswan Dam. Today, ancient Egypt may have lost some of its mystery but its fascination is as strong as ever. And the more we learn, the greater is our admiration for its remarkable achievements.

The British Egyptologist Howard Carter examines the coffin of King Tutankhamun, complete with mummy, which he had discovered in 1922.

'Some men say that they be sepulchres of great lords, that were sometime, but that is not true.'

A false idea of the pyramids in Sir John Mandeville's *Voyage*, written in the fourteenth century.

Archaeology and inscription

Our knowledge of ancient Egyptian civilization comes mainly from two sources: archaeology and inscriptions.

There are three reasons why so much of archaeological interest has remained. First, the Egyptians built their large monuments in durable stone. Second, materials last much longer in Egypt's hot, dry climate than they do in wetter lands. Finally, the Egyptian custom of placing everyday objects in a grave led to their being preserved for all time.

Egyptian writing appears as inscriptions carved on stone and as writing on papyrus. Lots of pieces of papyrus have survived, but they are very fragile and often just fragments which are hard to piece together.

Working out the puzzle

Finding out about ancient Egypt is like assembling a jigsaw with lots of the pieces missing. Historians use the pieces they have to work out what the missing bits looked like. It is not easy! For example, we are never told what the relationship between men and women was like.

The Great Sphinx at Giza, south of Cairo. For centuries this huge statue of a man with a lion's body has cast a spell of wonder over all who see it.

We have to make an intelligent guess from legal records, statues and paintings.

The biggest problem is fixing dates. We have lists of kings, stating how many years each one reigned. But Egyptian years, unlike ours, depended on the moon. Moreover, the Egyptians had no calendar of years, so we don't know when each king reigned. All we can do is work out rough dates from references to the position of Sirius, the Dog Star.

The Rosetta Stone

For centuries, historians' knowledge of ancient Egypt was limited by their inability to understand hieroglyphics. Then, in 1799, a Frenchman discovered an ancient stone set in a wall in Rosetta (Rashid), near Alexandria. Carved on the stone were three types of writing: Greek, hieroglyphics and demotic (a later form of hieroglyphics).

Historians worked out that the three types of writing were different versions of the same text. The hieroglyphic text was a translation of the Greek. So, because they understood Greek, they were slowly able to translate the hieroglyphics. At last, historians were able to read the language of ancient Egypt and unravel more of the secrets of this magnificent and intriguing civilization.

Not until historians learned how to read hieroglyphic writing in the nineteenth century did we realize that these glazed pottery vases are decorated with the name of King Rameses II.

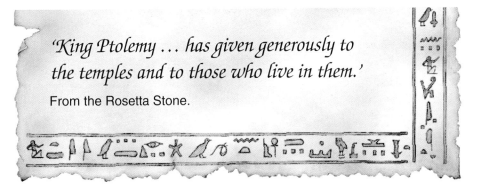

'King Ptolemy ... has given generously to the temples and to those who live in them.'

From the Rosetta Stone.

Glossary

Adobe
Mud bricks used for building.

Amulet
Good luck charm. They were either representations of gods or goddesses (or their symbols), or hieroglyphs for words such as 'beauty' or 'life'.

Apprentice
Young person employed in the workshop of an expert to learn their craft.

Archaeologist
Someone who studies the past by examining physical remains, usually through excavation.

Barter
Exchange goods instead of buying and selling for money.

Bronze
Metal made by mixing copper and tin.

Deity
Another word for a god or goddess.

Delta
When a river spreads into several channels as it nears the sea.

Drought
Time of no rainfall and severe water shortage.

Dynasty
Ruling family.

Empire
Several lands under the rule of an emperor, empress or pharaoh.

Faience
Glazed coloured pottery.

Ferment
Change liquid to produce alcohol.

Hieroglyph
Ancient Egyptian form of writing that used symbols rather than an alphabet.

Inscription
Short piece of writing, often carved in stone.

Kohl
Black eyeliner.

Literate
Able to read and write.

Papyrus
Tough river reed. The Egyptians made its stems into a type of paper, called papyrus.

Pharaoh
Originally the king's 'great house'. Later, it was used to mean the person from the great house – the king himself.

Potion
Magical or medicinal mixture.

Renaissance
Development of arts in Western Europe, from the late fourteenth century onwards, associated with renewed interest in ancient Greece and Rome.

Scribe
Someone skilled at writing.

Senet
Ancient Egyptian board game.

Vizier
Important adviser and minister in the king's household.

Time Line

All date are BC and approximate only.

7000–5500	Neolithic Age.
5500–3150	Predynastic Period. Badarians settle in Upper Egypt. Hieroglyphic writing begins.
3150–2690	Archaic Period (Dynasties 1 and 2).
2690–2180	Old Kingdom (Dynasties 3–6). Sphinx and Great Pyramid at Giza built. Continual wars against Nubians and Libyans.
2180–2055	First Intermediate Period (Dynasties 7–10).
2055–1650	Middle Kingdom (Dynasties 11–14). King Mentuhotep reunites Egypt.
1650–1550	Second Intermediate Period (Dynasties 15–17). Bronze used.
1550–1070	New Kingdom (Dynasties 18–20). Reigns of Hatshepsut, Thutmose III and Tutankhamun. Tombs built in the Valley of the Kings. Temple of Amenhotep III built at Luxor. Reigns of Rameses II and III.
1070–747	Third Intermediate Period (Dynasties 21–24). Conquest by Nubians.
747–332	Late Period (Dynasties 25–30). Conquest by Assyrians and Persians.
332–305	Macedonian Dynasty. Conquest by Alexander the Great.

Further Information

Books for children:
An Ancient Egyptian Child by J. Fletcher (Working White, 1999).
Ancient Egypt by K. Hayden (World Books, 1998).
Exploring Ancient Egypt by John Malam (Evans, 1999).
Women in Ancient Egypt by Fiona Macdonald (Belitha Press, 1999).
A Visitor's Guide to Ancient Eygpt by L. Sims (Usborne, 2000)
People Who Made History in Ancient Egypt by J. Shuter (Hodder Wayland, 2000).
The Ancient Egyptians by J. Shuter (Hodder Wayland, 1998).
The Awesome Egyptians by T. Deary (Scholastic, 1997).

Books for older readers:
Ancient Egypt edited by D. Silverman (Duncan Baird, 1997).
Atlas of Ancient Egypt by J. Baines and J. Malek (Facts on File, 1983).
Everyday Life in Egypt in the Days of Rameses the Great by P. Montet (University of Pennsylvania, 1998).
The British Museum of Ancient Egypt by S. Quirke and J. Spencer (Thames and Hudson, 1996).
The Egyptians by C. Aldred (Thames and Hudson, 1998).

Internet sites:
Browse with care! While there are some excellent sites on ancient Egypt, there are also some inaccurate ones. You may like to start with these:
http://www.guardians.net/egypt
http://www2.sptimes.com/egyptcredit.4.html
http://www.clpgh.org/cmnh/exhibits/egypt
http://www.ancientegypt.co.uk/menu.html

Index